The Love of Destiny

The Sacred and the Profane in Germanic Polytheism

by Dan McCoy

The deer were bounding like blown leaves
Under the smoke in front of the roaring wave of the
brushfire;
I thought of the smaller lives that were caught.
Beauty is not always lovely; the fire was beautiful, the
terror
Of the deer was beautiful; and when I returned
Down the black slopes after the fire had gone by, an
eagle
Was perched on the jag of a burnt pine,
Insolent and gorged, cloaked in the folded storms of his
shoulders.
He had come from far off for the good hunting
With fire for his beater to drive the game; the sky was
merciless
Blue, and the hills merciless black,
The sombre-feathered great bird sleepily merciless
between them.
I thought, painfully, but the whole mind,
The destruction that brings an eagle from heaven is
better than mercy.

- Robinson Jeffers, *Fire on the Hills*

Table of Contents

Introduction

The very word "sacred" makes people uncomfortable nowadays. "Our age is the age of science, modernism and postmodernism, a purely utilitarian economics, and the great leveler of globalization; what use could we possibly have for the 'sacred?'" they might say. To which I would reply that our age clings so fervently to these dubious endeavors precisely *because* the nihilism and objectification manifested by them are, paradoxically, sacred to most of us. This is paradoxical only because we think of the sacred in the terms bequeathed to us by the classical monotheistic religions we have been all too eager to shake off. That is, for something to be sacred, it must, in the monotheistic view, be objectively true and provide an absolute code of morality. It necessarily involves some doctrine of the One True Something and the one right way to live. While it has been sensible and in many ways helpful to reject this view, one cannot help but ask how much we have actually moved beyond it if we still insist on speaking of the sacred and the profane in monotheistic terms. Even if we no longer advocate the particulars of the worldview of Moses, Paul, or Mohammed, their worldview is still the reference point by which we define our own, like rebellious teenagers whose identity circles around what they oppose. The task before us, then, is to craft worldviews and ways of life that are *not*

9

monotheistic or dependent on monotheism, and which, instead, affirm the scandalous plurality of existence and its animating forces, as well as the perspectival and relational - rather than "objective" or "subjective" - character of truths and values. This would be a revival of polytheism, one that goes beyond the reintroduction of the outer forms of ancient polytheisms that so far have dominated Neopaganism and related movements. The French theologian Alain de Benoist and others have rightly pointed out that these "folkloric reconstructions" can be little more than anachronistic if unaccompanied by a reconstruction of the worldview that constitutes the heart of polytheism. The *spirit* of polytheism, its affirmation of the sublimely disturbing polyvalence of life and its courageousness in the face of that polyvalence, has the power to shock us out of our satanic torpor and provide us with truly viable alternatives to the things to which so many of us so desperately seek alternatives.

I say "worldviews," "ways of life," and "alternatives" in the plural because there cannot, by definition, be only one answer to the problems we have inherited with monotheism. Such a response would be, in and of itself, monotheistic, just like the popular banter about how everything is "subjective" rather than "objective." Rather, we need as many different polytheisms as there are people, peoples, communities, and landbases.

This task necessitates, first and foremost, a new way of speaking, because as Audre Lorde wrote in *Poetry is Not a Luxury*, "Poetry is the way we help give name to the nameless so it can be thought." A new way of speaking is what I have attempted to provide in this essay by introducing the rich vocabulary of polytheism. This will necessarily include an overview of the worldview and language of monotheism so that the reader can understand what is truly at stake in this "revaluation of all values," as Nietzsche called it. But after discussing the dominant historical currents of Judaism, Greek rationalism, Christianity, and science, I move as quickly as possible to the ancient polytheism of the Germanic peoples, and end, I hope, with one possible answer that actually addresses the depth of the question of what the heart of polytheism really is, not just with reference to monotheism, but on its own terms - a radical redefinition of what constitutes the sacred and what constitutes the profane.

I could have chosen the historical polytheism of countless societies from across the world to illustrate the main points of this work, and, like Heraclitus's river, each of those other hypothetical essays would have been extraordinarily different and yet somehow the same. But I have chosen to base this work off of the polytheism of my own northern European ancestors because they are the people with whom I am most familiar, and because, since they are my ancestors, I have a certain special fondness for them. I hope that readers will look to their own distant (or, in some cases, not so distant) ancestors for inspiration, whoever their ancestors happen to be.

Who were the Germanic peoples, then? They - we - are some of the indigenous peoples of northern Europe, along with the Celts, Sámi, Finns, and others. Most of the inhabitants of modern-day England, Sweden, Norway, Denmark, Germany, Austria, Iceland, the Netherlands, Australia, the United States, and other countries have at least some Germanic blood in them. The traditional Germanic religion was centrally concerned with the concept of destiny (Old English *wyrd* and Old Norse *urðr*), and involved the veneration of deities such as Odin (Old Norse *Óðinn*, Old English *Woden*, Old High German *Wotan*, from Proto-Germanic **Woðanaz*), Thor (Old Norse *Þórr*, Old English *Þunor*, Old High German *Donar*, from Proto-Germanic **Þunraz*), and Freya/Frigg (Old Norse *Freyja* or *Frigg*, Old English *Frig*, Old High German *Frija*, from Proto-Germanic **Frijo*). Since the Icelanders resisted the incursions of Christianity the longest and prized literariness so highly, most of the information about the pre-Christian worldview of the Germanic peoples that survived into the present day comes from Icelandic sources written in Old Norse in the Viking Age and Middle Ages. Unfortunately, this information is still highly fragmentary, but it is enough to provide some glimpses into an astonishingly beautiful and powerful worldview. For this reason, proper nouns from ancient Germanic languages are almost invariably given in Old

Norse in this essay. Some prior knowledge of Norse mythology will certainly be helpful in understanding this piece, but it is by no means necessary, and even a reader with no background whatsoever in these topics - or, worse, a miseducation about them through popular culture - will be able to keep up. To make this easier, I have included a glossary of Old Norse terms at the end of the essay. Rather than anglicize the names, I have left them in Old Norse in order to preserve more of their original, and to us strangely "other," character, which forces the reader to approach these words and the figures and concepts they denote with fewer preconceptions. Most letters in Old Norse are pronounced more or less the same as they are in modern English, but there are a few exceptions and a few characters that the English language has lost in the long transition from Old English to modern English:

j	like modern English "y" as in "your"
þ	soft "th" as in "thorn"
ð	hard "th" as in "those"
ó	long "o" as in "bone"
é	"ay" as in "day"
í	"ee" as in "feet"
á	"ow" as in "blowse"
ú	"oo" as in "food"
ý	"ee" as in "feet"
ö	same as modern German ö
æ	"i" as in "high"

œ   "i" as in "high"
ei   "ay" as in "day"

The reader will no doubt notice that I have refrained from citing sources. This is intentional. As Charles Olson said, "Form is never more than an extension of content," and a work that attempts to dismantle the objective-subjective dichotomy must, if it is to be effective, demonstrate a way of writing that blurs the line between "objective" or scholarly writing and "subjective" or creative writing. Citing sources seems uselessly petty in a work that is not primarily concerned with factual claims, but rather with mythic visions that contextualize any and all facts. Citing sources is a defensive mode of writing, one that tries to protect a vision from criticism by seeking support for it in the consensus reality of its day. What I am presenting here, however, draws much more heavily from the oracular mode of writing exemplified by the great mythical poetry of the ancients, such as Homer or the Poetic Edda (or even the Bible or certain passages of Descartes, for that matter), works that were perceived to be "self-evident" because they were sacred and divinely inspired. If readers wish to criticize the ideas presented in this work, they must criticize the ideas themselves on their own terms rather than adopt the disingenuous tactic of surreptitiously challenging the ideas by ostensibly challenging the facts that surround them. Besides, there are few factual statements in this work. All of them are corroborated by the works in the bibliography, and should not be especially difficult to verify for readers who know how to use the Internet and are curious about the origin of a particular quote or historical assertion.

One final word of caution: the terms "monotheism" and "polytheism" are employed in a somewhat original way, and should not be taken too literally as merely referring, respectively, to an intellectual belief in one god and an intellectual belief in many gods. As this work attempts to show, the belief in a single god (or, for that matter, a unitary absence of divinity) is an outgrowth of a much more comprehensive worldview that I am here calling "monotheism," just as the comprehensive worldview that I am calling "polytheism" lends itself to the belief in a plurality of deities but cannot be reduced to such a belief. Thus, I am certainly not saying that all of the present-day adherents of historically monotheistic religions embody all of the flaws that I point to in the monotheistic worldview, nor that present-day adherents of reconstructions of historically polytheistic religions embody all of the characteristics that I point to as comprising a typically polytheistic worldview. Far from it. I have personally known many Christians, for example, who are "better" polytheists than many of the "pagans" I have known. Furthermore, I would be the last person in the world to assert that traditionally monotheistic religions such as Christianity, Judaism, Islam, or science should be done away with if there are still those who find them useful and beautiful for themselves; rather, as a polytheist, I unreservedly affirm the legitimacy of their spirituality alongside my own, provided, of course, that they extend the same tolerance and respect to me and my own perspective. I will criticize what I find to be the shortcomings of monotheism, and I am sure that monotheists will in turn criticize what they find to be the shortcomings of polytheism as I present it here. As long as the devotees of Zeus or Artemis do not try to stamp out the worship of Aphrodite or Pan, nothing is amiss.

I.
Prologue

Polytheism and Monotheism

The world is far less benevolent, and far more callous, than we often feel that it should be. Episodic traumas such as the untimely death of one's loved ones, injury, sickness, abuse, and war punctuate a tale whose uncertain plot is defined by the necessity of constant killing and toiling in order to obtain the proverbial essentials in life: food, clothing, and shelter, which are essential precisely because of their warding off the yet more malevolent presences of hunger and cold. Once obtained, our hold on what we have is precarious and fleeting. Survival and health depend on luck, hard-won skill, and what might as well be called magic. Our knowledge is thwarted by contradiction after contradiction and anomaly after anomaly. While the plot of our lives may be impossible to predict, the ending is as sure as it is calamitous: we, along with everyone we have ever known, will die and be eaten by other beings who are themselves, through no choice of their own, swimming in susceptibility to an infinity of great and small pains. When the story ends, it begins again and repeats itself throughout eternity. While even the most wretched of lives have their pleasures and perhaps even joys, the harrowing elements are at least as formidable as those pleasanter ones.

What are we to do in the face of this injustice, this amorality, this blasphemous vulnerability that constitutes the basic precondition of life?

For the past three thousand years, swaths of our species have answered this question by attempting to reconstitute, to reform, to "save" the world according to a set of absolutist principles. These principles are ostensibly never derived from an ordinary perceptual engagement with the world of which we are a part, but rather from an "otherworld" that is cleanly and coldly separate from our world. This is monotheism, the moralistic rejection of the world as we experience it as entirely and hopelessly profane, bereft of any meaning of its own, in favor of this "otherworld," which is the sole abode of anything that can rightly be called "sacred." A cowardice that refuses to meet the world on its own terms is complemented by a program of imperialistic conquest of the world to reshape its most basic elements according to the monotheist's image of a humanistic otherworld. Vitality and beauty are pushed aside by endless lists of "thou shalts" and "thou shalt nots" that have no room for them. This affront to life continues unabated in the scientific rationalism of our own day, which is perhaps the most thoroughly monotheistic of all of these religions.

But even among those peoples who have been bound under the spell of these attitudes the longest, the duration of the reign of monotheism and morality has been scarcely more than a blink compared to humankind's vast and venerable history of polytheism. What characterizes this other approach to life, which the overwhelming majority of our ancestors - no matter who your ancestors are - have enacted?

It would be laughable to suppose that the differences between monotheism and polytheism consist of a mere multiplication of the number of deities. Where monotheism is a moral worldview, polytheism is a *sacral* one. The sacred is not remote from the world; it is the very essence *of* the world. All that is profane speaks to us of the sacred if we listen attentively enough, for the world we inhabit is the very flesh of spirit, its organic manifestation. The plural character of life, which mocks the moralist's attempt to reduce it to an absolutely good and true side and an absolutely evil and false side, is an expression of that which prevails on the divine plane, with its plurality of gods and goddesses. The polytheist does not wring his hands over the struggles and contradictions with which he is confronted, but confronts them in turn. Her overcoming of the world and being overcome by the world is the sacred's overcoming of itself. She stares unflinchingly into its terror, its pain, its ruthlessness, and its unfairness - and, understanding that these are inseparably coupled with prosperity, joy, pleasure, and love, she is capable of seeing the sublime at work everywhere and of affirming the whole without exception.

II.

The Origins

and

Worldview of

Monotheism

The Hebrews

Over the course of the first millennium BCE, the traditional polytheism of a confederation of nomadic tribes in the deserts of the Middle East gave way to one of the two first monotheistic systems. One of the countless gods who were worshipped by the Israelites gradually became more and more prominent, abandoning his consort Asherah, declaring himself to be the only deity worthy of the attention of his "chosen people," and eventually proclaiming that he was the only true god, beside whom all other gods and goddesses were nothing more than imposters and demons.

The factual accuracy of the tales that comprise the Hebrew Bible is inconsequential for our purposes here. What matters to us is the *mythology* of these texts. How did the first Jewish monotheists perceive themselves, their god, and their place in the world? What was sacred to them, and what was the relationship between the sacred and the profane?

When the monotheistic revolution had been completed around the time of the Hebrews' exile in Babylon, Yahweh or Elohim had become a being radically unlike the gods and goddesses of the polytheistic peoples who surrounded the Hebrews. He was no animating power of some particular aspect of the human and more-than-human world - no, Yahweh was a Supreme Being who was completely *other than* the world. He was omniscient, omnipotent, and omnibenevolent, and had created this world singlehandedly and from the outside. The world was an artifact that received none of Yahweh's essence, like a shoe made by a shoemaker. As 1 Kings 19:11 says, "And behold, the Lord passed by, and a great and strong wind rent the mountains, and brake in pieces the rocks before the Lord; but the Lord was not in the wind: and after the wind an earthquake; but the Lord was not in the earthquake: and after the earthquake a fire; but the Lord was not in the fire..." His creation of the world happened at one particular moment in history, and thereafter he was to reveal himself only in particular historical events. Where the cycles of the more-than-human world had been some of the most powerful revelations of the polytheistic deities formerly worshipped by the Hebrews, only their own linear history was now (potentially) sacred to them.

This was because the lone component of the world that *had* received a spiritual essence was humanity, who was created "in the image of Elohim," according to the Book of Genesis. Being invested with a modicum of that which made Yahweh unique, humanity was not truly a part of the world at all, but, like Yahweh himself, belonged Somewhere Else.

Thus began the dichotomization of life into a "good" half and an "evil" half. On the good side stood Yahweh and humankind, and opposite them, like a rival army, stood the more-than-human world. Christianity inherited this impassible conceptual rift from Judaism, and science from Christianity. And so we have, on the good side and the evil side, respectively, culture and nature, spirit and matter, the mind and the body, the objective and the subjective, the rational and the irrational, being and becoming, free will and instinct, and, in Sartre's formulation, essence and existence.

Morality was the inevitable consequence of this binary cosmology. The sacred was no longer *within* the world, but resided in another world and was even *against* the world, and therefore had to be forcibly injected into the world from without. Actions were no longer to be evaluated based on desire and practicality, the honest and elegant standards of thrushes, wolves, and cedars. Instead, they were to be evaluated based on how well or how badly they facilitated the reform of the world as dictated by the One God.

The first moral command was issued by Yahweh before he had even fashioned humans: "And Elohim said, 'Let us make man in our image, after our likeness: and let them have dominion over the fish of the sea, and over the fowl of the air, and over the cattle, and over all the earth, and over every creeping thing that creepeth upon the earth'" (Genesis 1:26). The subjugation of the more-than-human world, its being brought into conformity with the "image" of Yahweh, was now the imperative of the righteous. What we today call "civilization" had existed long before the advent of monotheism, and began as a straightforward, practical, and probably non-ideological adaptation to a changing climate. The transition from hunting and gathering to husbandry and

27

agriculture had been slow and seamless, so much so that one has to wonder if the many generations of intermediary collectors and horticulturalists had even thought of themselves as doing anything fundamentally differently than their recent ancestors at each step along the way. The same can be said of the builders of the first permanent camps, villages, towns, and cities. Each successive generation thought of their way of life as "how our people live," just as all other peoples had their own somewhat unique ways of life and all other species had theirs. For the first monotheists, however, "civilization" was coterminous with nothing but the will of Yahweh and his earthly servants. It signified a radical break with the rest of the world, one of the means by which the human faithful impose Yahweh's commandments upon a recalcitrant universe. For the Hebrews, humanity was now categorically distinct from other species, and when Yahweh's wrath turned against cities like Sodom and Gomorrah, it was for their refusal to *extend* their "dominion over all the earth" to include matters of human-to-human relations, as we shall see. If we are to believe the modern heirs of this vision, the face of God must look much like the New York City skyline.

"Dominion over all the earth" had many more ramifications for human behavior - or, at least, the shape that human behavior was *supposed* to take. To be fit to dominate the earth, Yahweh's followers had to dominate themselves, to render themselves unconditionally obedient to this coarse tyrant of a god: "Thou shalt have no other gods before me. Thou shalt not make unto thee any graven image, or any likeness of any thing that is in heaven above, or that is in the earth beneath, or that is in the water under the earth. Thou shalt not bow down thyself to them, nor serve them, for I the Lord thy God am a jealous God" (Exodus 20:3-5). Adultery, theft, murder, lying, blasphemy, the obtainment of "knowledge of good and evil," and, ironically, covetousness, were "idolatry" - lacking a legitimately divine archetype - and therefore intolerable and deserving of nothing but to be stamped out at any cost.

Upon receiving the moral Law and becoming its appointed enforcers, the Hebrews occupied the land of Canaan and slew its idolatrous inhabitants, making a point to spare no man, woman, or child. As their reward for perpetrating the world's first true genocide, Yahweh granted them the Canaanites' "land of milk and honey" as their own.

The Greeks

Meanwhile, to the west, the Greeks were succumbing to a monotheism of their own, one which was to prove no less influential than that of the Israelites.

Its first stirrings can be traced in the philosophy of Socrates, whose systematic questioning of traditional Greek polytheism amounted to a systematic profaning of that archaic religion. The sacred is that which, by definition, cannot be questioned, but rather overwhelms and fills with awe. To subject an idea or a tradition to a skeptical and purely mundane method of analysis is to drag it into the realm of the mundane and profane, to cast it as something plain, unexceptional, and uninspiring. The Athenian government, of course, repaid the efforts of their "gadfly" with a cup of hemlock.

In many ways, Socrates represented a proto-monotheistic disposition to life. For example, when asked why he spent his time in towns rather than in the hills and forests like other wise men, he declared, "Fields and trees will not teach me anything, but men do." With these few words, he sweepingly declared the entirety of the more-than-human world to be without sense or sentience, an idea which his animistic peers evidently greeted with derision. Socrates's role in the creation of Greek monotheism was mostly a negative one, however - that is, by profaning the old system, he enabled his successors to craft philosophical systems that were not particularly dependent upon the polytheism of their people.

The first to actively create such a system was Socrates's ablest student, Plato. Plato's cosmology retained something of the mystical and sacral character of the polytheism of his forebears, such as the high value it granted to intuition and revelation and its perception of the particulars of the visible world as embodying an invisible and more eternal dimension of life. Nevertheless, it also introduced a number of innovations that were decidedly monotheistic, dualistic, and moralistic (which are, as we have seen with the Hebrews, three ways of saying the same thing).

For Plato, this eternal realm at the heart of life was the world of Ideas. Any oak tree in the visible world was a dim, corrupted semblance of the incorporeal Idea or archetype of an oak tree. The foremost of these Ideas, the archetype of archetypes, was the Good - "good" in an unabashedly moral sense. The Good, in turn, was an emanation of the One, the creator of all life, which should remind us of nothing quite so much as the omnibenevolence attributed to Yahweh. The world of the Ideas was pure Being, utterly static and unchanging in its perfect Good-ness, as opposed to the dynamic cyclicality that characterizes the world of spirit in polytheistic worldviews. The sensual world, in contrast to the placid world of Ideas, was a world of Becoming, of chaotic and wayward flux. Corporeality was merely a distortion of the incorporeal Ideas, no longer a theophany in its own right.

Unsurprisingly, Plato harbored a deep-seated distrust of the senses, as can perhaps be seen most vividly in his famous cave allegory. Human perception, unaided by (Platonic) philosophy, was compared to sitting bound within a cave facing one wall, with fires burning behind one's back. One sees only shadows cavorting on the wall, never laying eyes upon the things that actually cast these shadows. The (Platonic) philosopher is one who somehow frees himself from his chains and from the cave and flees to the sunlit world outside, where he can behold things as they truly are. Here was a sharp distinction between the world of perception and another *true* world, a position which found its counterpart in Plato's morality of self-abnegation and abstinence from worldly pleasures.

While Plato's philosophy was a partial break from traditional Greek polytheism, the system devised by his pupil Aristotle was a near-total one. The cornerstone of Aristotle's philosophy, the unspoken assumption upon which all of his other foundational assumptions rested, was the enshrining of the total profaneness and meaninglessness of the world as a sacred truth in and of itself. Plato had constrained the role of the sacred in his philosophy, yes, but Aristotle attempted to dispense with it altogether, relegating it to a hidden position at the heart of his doctrines, but utterly banished from the exhibited character of his doctrines themselves. This intellectual sleight-of-hand enabled him to vaunt his proto-empirical method for obtaining knowledge as more rational, more "objective," than the methods of his competitors, and especially that of his own mentor. If Aristotle is considered to be the "philosopher of common sense" today, it is only because we have adopted his perspective so thoroughly that the compelling alternatives are almost literally unthinkable.

Plato's worldview, like that of his polytheistic ancestors, left wide margins for inspiration by the gods and goddesses (or, in Plato's case, the One) whose existence encompasses but transcends our own. He would have agreed with Heidegger that, at least with regard to the thoughts that form the bedrock upon which a philosophical landscape can thrive, "We do not come to thoughts. They come to us." Visions of ultimate reality were a "spark" implanted in the "soul" by these greater forces, an instance of communion with the more-than-human world.

The polytheistic or Platonic conception of the mind might be imagined as a forest or a steppe, with an openness onto the reciprocity and flow of the universe no different from the openness of a more tangible land. Aristotle, however, effectively created the modern notion of the "individual," cut off from these channels of give-and-take, with his assertion that all thought occurs within the human mind alone. The Aristotelian mind was a locked room, full of still and stale air, a pure *internality* against which the only *externality* was of a purely physical sort. There was nothing of the sacred in either the internal or the external worlds, only the profaneness that was by its very nature susceptible to Socratic analysis. As we shall see, statements at this - let us call it what it is - *mythic* level cannot be defended by reason; a myth is a myth precisely because of its impenetrability by reason, and this aloofness from questioning is what marks the sacredness of a myth. Once again, paradoxically, the relentless profanation that characterized Aristotle's proto-empiricism was rooted in what was, for him, nothing short of a sacred truth.

Aristotle's epistemological method consisted of automatically denying any myths besides this one, attempting to artificially exclude the intuition from the process of perception, leaving only the amputated senses to perform a proto-scientific mode of "observation," and then arriving at general principles through aggregating these observations. These new, objectifying principles would be inherently truer than the more consciously inspired views they replaced. While this was virtually the diametrical opposite of Plato's epistemology, it was no less otherworldly, and indeed even more so. At least Plato had retained some of the animist's conscious participation in the more-than-human world. For Aristotle, there was to be no such thing. The seeker after knowledge was to be a detached observer, a spectator at an arena, whose access to truth was in direct proportion to his isolation from the objects of his study, and, by extension, the world of which they were a part. Continuity and communion were hopelessly mired in "subjectivity."

In Aristotle's "objective" and objectified cosmology, polytheistic concepts like Fate, which gave an order and coherence to the world *from within* and therefore could not be observed empirically, had to be rejected out of hand. In its place, Aristotle substituted the concept of cause and effect to explain how and why events occur. One happening mechanically caused other happenings in linear sequences that could be fully grasped by the locked-up human mind. Even Aristotle's god was described in these terms: he was the sole creator, the First Cause, the Unmoved Mover who gave form to inert matter. His - or, rather, "its," since Aristotle used the neuter pronoun - forming of matter took place at one specific time in the past, and did not repeat cyclically. "Its thinking is a thinking on thinking," having no need to concern itself with the vicissitudes and tumult of worldly life, and, of course, it was purely "Good."

The Christians

Despite the claims of many Christians that their religion is a radical departure from all others, past and present, it was actually a simple and direct continuation of the Jewish and post-Socratic Greek philosophy of the first millennium BCE that we have already considered. All of Christianity's essential features - its one god, its cold separation of "nature" on the one hand and the human and divine world on the other, its moralizing attitude toward life - were already in place hundreds of years before the first gospels were written. Nietzsche's characterization of Christianity as "Platonism for the masses" is, in most respects, a highly fitting one.

Even its doctrine of a messiah was stolen from Jewish tradition. The Hebrew prophets had long spoken of a savior who would deliver them from their earthly bondage, first to the Babylonians and then to the Romans, and restore them to their former glory as a "chosen people" exempt from the suffering and uncertainties of life in proportion to their obedience to Yahweh. Jesus - again, as a mythical figure, leaving aside questions of factual accuracy - was just such a person. His otherworldly salvation - "Not as the world giveth, give I unto you" (John 14:27) - was, as we have seen, an outgrowth of the monotheistic dream of aloofness from the world and its vexations, as was his morality of self-denial and conversion. His being the incarnation of a god would have meant nothing to the surrounding polytheistic society, who perceived the entire world to be the incarnation of hordes of gods and goddesses, and his promise of salvation would have struck them as mendacious and fainthearted at best.

Why, then, was Christianity so successful? It gained its first inroads into Roman society by valorizing the squalor of the disenchanted masses - the "poor in spirit" - and promising them a "kingdom" in return for their misery (Matthew 5:3). When its popularity grew to the point that it was one of the most prominent of the various foreign cults that were sweeping the Empire as it collapsed, the emperors saw its potential to lend Rome's increasingly desperate imperial ambitions the status of a holy crusade, turning practical or aesthetic aims into *moral* ones. After its installment as the state religion of Rome and the completion of the collapse of the Empire itself, the Church had become an institution with sufficient *worldly* power to embark on crusades throughout the neighboring lands, converting the rulers and nobility over the course of the next several centuries with political and economic incentives, and, failing that, the sword. The sentiments and allegiances of the general populace of much of Europe, however, remained polytheistic and animistic well into the fifteenth century and beyond. It took nothing short of the combined force of the Reformation, the witch trials, and the Scientific Revolution to stamp out those last vestiges of a nobler and more beautiful time.

The Scientists

Just as Christianity was a straightforward outgrowth of Judaism and Greek rationalism, so science was a straightforward outgrowth of all three. Of course, science parades as a timeless and "objective" method for acquiring knowledge with an equally "objective" body of doctrines it has amassed as the fruits of this quest, but these are circular justifications that appeal to science's own core assumptions - its myths. Science is nothing more and nothing less than the religion of the post-Christian modern world, and is only unquestionable inasmuch as we perceive it to be *sacred*.

More specifically, science is a quintessentially monotheistic religion, one whose origin, as with the other varieties of monotheism we have considered, lies in a profound hatred and fear of the world in which we actually live, and a moralistic desire to "save" the world and bring it into conformity with a hypothetical and more tolerable "otherworld."

The early modern prophets of science made this intention very clear. Echoing the first moral command in the Book of Genesis, René Descartes, the founder of modern rationalism, declared that humans are to be "masters and possessors of nature," and that there is no idea "which is so apt to make weak characters stray from the path of virtue as the idea that the souls of animals are the same as our own, and that in consequence we have no more to fear or to hope for after this life than have the flies or ants." Or in the words of Robert Boyle, who "discovered" Boyle's Law, "The veneration, wherewith men are imbued for what they call nature, has been a discouraging impediment to the empire of man over the inferior creatures of God." Francis Bacon, the founder of modern empiricism, who mused with sadistic glee over the prospect of "putting [nature] on the rack and extracting her secrets," proclaimed, "I am come in very truth leading you to Nature with all her children to bind her to your service and make her your slave. ... The mechanical inventions of recent years do not merely exert a gentle guidance over Nature's courses, they have the power to conquer and subdue her, to shake her to her foundations." Isaac Newton reiterated these Christian intentions: "When I wrote my treatise about our system [*Philosophiæ Naturalis Principia Mathemetica*] I had an eye upon such principles as might work with considering men for the belief of a Deity; and

38

nothing can rejoice me more than to find it useful for that purpose."

The first modern scientists appropriated Aristotle's method of detached observation of "objects." Just as with Aristotle, this enabled them to hold themselves at a position of artificial remove from the world and to stunt and narrow their perception - this wild, syncopated dance between perceiver and perceived and between the intuition and the senses - until they saw nothing but resources for the construction of "the Dominion of Man over the Universe," in Bacon's words, the re-creation of the world "in the image of" their otherworld.

In *Beyond Good and Evil*, Nietzsche insightfully wrote, "Gradually it has become clear to me what every philosophy so far has been: namely, the personal confession of its author and a kind of involuntary and unconscious memoir; also that the moral (or immoral) intentions in every philosophy constituted the real germ of life from which the whole plant had grown." The first heralds of science made no secret about the moral seeds out of which the truth claims of their philosophy arose, and only if we understand these "germs" can we understand the "plant" as a whole. What, then, were the most central of these claims about the basic constitution of reality - the sapling, as it were?

Then and now, the system of thought instituted by Descartes, Bacon, Boyle, and their compatriots has been called the "mechanical philosophy," because it posits that the universe that is to become the "Dominion of Man" is nothing more than a machine, an inert object that can consequently be observed objectively from without. No divinity, no spirit, no will, no agency, no consciousness, resides within the more-than-human world. The perennially disenchanted Descartes, finding intolerable the notion that anything in the world could be explained without positing purely corporeal causes, totally devoid of mind and thought, wrote, "There exist no occult forces in stones or plants, no amazing and marvelous sympathies and antipathies, in fact there exists nothing in the whole of nature which cannot be explained in terms of purely corporeal causes, totally devoid of mind and thought." He went on to say, "[Animals] have no mind at all, and it is nature which acts in them according to the disposition of their organs, just as a clock, which is only composed of wheels and weights, is able to tell the hours and measure the time." Similarly, for Nicolas Malebranche, nonhuman animals "eat without pleasure, they cry without pain, they grow without knowing it; they desire nothing, they fear nothing, they know nothing." All of these conceptions would have been impossible without the precedent established in Genesis, where the world was an artifact created by a god who remained separate from his creation at the opposite side of an unbridgeable gap.

Only humanity had anything that could rightly be called will, consciousness, or spirit. Since humanity and the world were representatives of the opposing principles of a dichotomy, human "subjectivity" or "free will" was a corollary of the mechanical, objectified nature of the rest of the world. This, too, was dependent on the mythology of Genesis; only humanity was "made in the image of God." It was also dependent on Aristotle's confinement of thought to the human mind, with no input from forces and beings outside of itself. "I think, therefore I am," a statement which Descartes felt to be a self-evident truth, is preposterous outside of this Christian-Aristotelian tradition. Remember the words of Heidegger: "We do not come to thoughts. They come to us."

But all of these curious suggestions were necessitated by the moral urgency of achieving "dominion over all the earth," "the Dominion of Man over the Universe."

The scientific method follows ineluctably from these myths. It is simply a reification of them. When the scientist uproots the subjects of his experiment from their proper worldly context, inserts them into an artificial, controlled environment designed to isolate certain variables that are *not* isolated in the original phenomena themselves, observes this simulation from a position of as much remove as possible, quantifies his observations based on predetermined conventions of statistical analysis, and then repeats this experiment as many times as necessary to remove any nuance of living particularity, what kind of knowledge does he actually gain? He obviously does not achieve any greater understanding of the phenomena in question on their own terms. Such would require abandoning his otherworldly detachment and immersing himself in the smarting throb of life within which these phenomena are themselves and not anything else. He would thereby come to know them as they are, tumbling through experience and participation, just as we do when we get to know another human being.

But science has always been unconcerned with the search for truth in and of itself; it cares for truth only inasmuch as it might facilitate science's program of "binding Nature to [our] service and making her [our] slave." Science's prophets said as much themselves. Bacon, in a recitation of the dogma of the mechanical philosophy, wrote, "Toward the effecting of works, all that man can do is to put together or put asunder natural bodies. The rest is done by nature [that is, mechanical laws] working within." He then went on to say, "Truth is revealed and established by the evidence of works [putting together and putting asunder natural bodies] rather than by disputation, or even sense." Taken together, these assertions declare that truth is determined *a priori* by the mechanical philosophy, which is, after all, what the scientific method is designed to reinforce. Robert Boyle made the same declaration when he wrote, "If the proposed agent be not intelligible and physical, it can never physically explain the phenomena; so if it be intelligible and physical, it will be reducible to matter and some or other of those only catholic [universal] affections of matter." These are statements of *myth* - and this realization does not, in and of itself, invalidate them. It does, however, invalidate the all-too-common misconception that science and myth are categorically distinct from one another, and shows, rather, that science is as deeply embedded in myth as any other worldview, and that myth cannot be tested scientifically.

When Richard Dawkins and other missionaries of science defend their religion by squawking over the fact that "science gets results" - or, in Dawkins's more precise formulation, "Science boosts its claims to truth by its spectacular ability to make matter and energy jump through hoops on command, and to predict what will happen and when" - they are tacitly admitting that the purpose of science is to secure these desired results, to *transform* the world "in the image of Elohim," or "Progress," or "Objectivity," or whatever other names these monotheists have for their god, and not, primarily, to obtain any kind of greater understanding of the world we inhabit. This does not, of course, mean that science is objectively *false*. The mythology of science, being a mythology, cannot be proven or disproven according to any standard outside of its own myths, for such a standard would have to be an objective one - and, as we have already begun to see and will soon see more fully, there is no such external standard by which a myth can be verified or discredited. "Objectivity" is "merely" that which, from the perspective of science, cannot be questioned. This perspective deems an idea to be "objectively true" if it is *sacred* within this perspective, and it dismisses as "subjective" any idea that it finds to be profane, especially if that idea menaces that which it holds sacred. Science is true inasmuch as it propels the monotheist's dream of "dominion over all the earth." Outside of that endeavor, however, its "findings" have value only inasmuch as they approach simple anecdotal evidence.

Of course, one could invoke many other examples to illustrate the character of monotheism - Islam, snarling do-gooderism, totalitarian political movements, etc. But these few examples should suffice to illustrate monotheism's most essential features. With them in mind, what does polytheism - and the indigenous polytheism of the Germanic tribes in particular - have to offer as an alternative?

III.

The Sacred and the Profane

Spirit and Flesh

From a polytheistic perspective, the visible world is not a negation of the invisible world of spirit, but its fulfillment. The words that William Blake chose to end *The Marriage of Heaven and Hell*, "Everything that lives is holy," apply to all that we perceive and experience, no matter how grand and luminous, no matter how vile and distressing.

In his unfinished masterpiece, *The Visible and the Invisible*, the French phenomenologist Maurice Merleau-Ponty wrote: "[Ideas] could not be given to us *as ideas* except in a carnal experience. It is not only that we would find in that carnal experience the *occasion* to think them; it is that they owe their authority, their fascinating, indestructible power, precisely to the fact that they are in transparency behind the sensible, or in its heart... [The idea] is the invisible *of* this world, that which inhabits this world, sustains it, and renders it visible." The intuition and imagination, far from being "subjective" and therefore of little to no consequence where the real is concerned, have an openness upon the real that equals that of the senses. The mythical beings, realms, and events that they perceive are not false or nonexistent simply because they elude the senses, but rather dwell within an ordinarily latent - and yet ultimately deeper - modality of the world. Nor should the senses be shunned, for that which they divulge is fastened to that which is divulged by the invisible components of perception. Perception's visible and invisible parts cannot be isolated from one another; both are integrated into a seamless whole. Such, at least, is how we are surely to understand the Roman historian Tacitus's description of the religion of the Germanic tribes: "Their holy places are the woods and groves, and they apply the names of gods to those hidden presences seen only by the eye of reverence."

Despite its origins in the Latin word *mater*, "mother," our modern word "matter" has been invested with connotations of inertness, insensitivity, barrenness. To call it "dead" would be to impart to it too much life - it was never living in the first place. Against this Cartesian tendency, Merleau-Ponty described the visible world as *flesh*, within which all of us visible beings are intertwining sinews.

There is a particular resonance with Germanic mythology in his choice of words. Before the world as we today know it had emerged, there was only the primordial chaos of Ginnungagap ("Great Abyss"). Ymir ("Scream"), the animating spirit of this void of undisturbed silence and darkness, was slain by Óðinn and his brothers Vili ("Will") and Vé ("Consecration"), who then crafted the visible world from his flesh. As it is recounted in the Eddic poem *Grímnismál*:

> *Ór Ymis holdi*
> *Var jörð of sköpuð,*
> *En ór sveita sær,*

Björg ór beinum,
Baðmr ór hári,
En ór hausi himinn.

En ór hans brám
Gerðu blíð regin
Miðgarð manna sonum,
En ór hans heila
Váru þau in harðmóðgu
Ský öll of sköpuð.

[From Ymir's hide
Was earth created,
Seas from sweat,
Peaks from bones,
Trees from hair,
And from his skull the sky.

And from his brows
Made these blithe powers
Shelters for the sons of men,
And from his brains
The dark and baleful
Clouds were all then strung.]

Ymir's tribe, the *Jötnar* or "devourers," are adept at
shapeshifting, as are the gods and goddesses themselves.
One never knows when a falcon might be an incarnation
of Frigg, a wolf an incarnation of Óðinn, or an eagle an

incarnation of Þjazi. Þórr's name means "Thunder," and Týr's comes from an Indo-European root that meant both "god" and "the blue sky." The elements are permeated with divinity to the point that they are truly the flesh of the gods. And when the various profane and partial manifestations of the gods in the fleshly world are perceived with the "eye of reverence," the profane reveals itself to be a vessel of the sacred, and, to quote Blake once more, you

See a world in a grain of sand
And a heaven in a wild flower
Hold infinity in the palm of your hand
And eternity in an hour.

Myth

The profane can be questioned, debated, proven, or disproven. If I were to claim that a particular species of plant were safe to be eaten if prepared a certain way, and you were to prepare the plant in exactly that way and got sick when you ate it, and your reaction could not be ascribed to an allergy or other such complicating factor, then my assertion about the plant's safety would be demonstrably false. Similarly, if I were to claim that a particular piece of legislation would have particular effects on the economy, and if, after a number of years of the law having been on the books and observed, if no such effects were felt, then my assertion about the legislation's consequences would be demonstrably false. Knowledge of such tangible things as edible plants and economics is profane knowledge.

The sacred, however, is sacred precisely because of its immunity to such demonstrations and proofs. Truths that belong to the realm of the sacred are *myths*, in the most exalted sense of the word.

Myths are truths that are known *a priori* - they are just "there" in our perception, more often than not so deeply entrenched that we are not even conscious of their presence. When a new myth is revealed to us, it arrives in a flash of ecstasy that overpowers us so completely that it would be all but unthinkable to question it. Such experiences come much more readily to some than to others. Most people are never given such a revelation, except, perhaps, at the moment of a religious conversion, and they are otherwise perfectly content with the myths that they inherited at birth. Among poets and philosophers, however, such experiences are so common that they seem practically a cliché from the outside. In any case, by whatever means it has arrived, once a myth becomes lodged in our perception it cannot be removed except by another myth.

The very phrase *a priori* is our modern equivalent of *in illo tempore*, a phrase used by the famous scholar of religions Mircea Eliade to refer to the "time before time" when the narrative myths of many polytheistic peoples from all over the earth are supposed to have taken place, such as the "distant time" of the Koyukon or the "dreamtime" of the Australian Aborigines. (This is in contrast to Judaism and Christianity, which mythologized history itself, much as does the modern notion of "Progress.") Just as this earliest, a-historical time established the fundamentals of life that now characterize our profane, historical time, so do the ideas that most modern people claim to know *a priori*, "just because." Take, for example, the idea that science is the surest path to truth. Science and truth are both ideas rather than tangible things, and these invisible things cannot, in and of themselves, be put to the test. The platitude that "science gets results" is no more of a *proof* of the universal validity of the mythology of science than the slenderness of the salmon's tail is proof that, *in illo tempore*, Þórr caught Loki by the tail while the latter was hiding from the other gods in the form of a salmon. Both are justifications offered after the fact, as a disingenuous attempt to convince others of the validity of one's own myths. They show, in their own roundabout way, the futility of striving to subject a myth to some sort of external standard of verification. Any number of other conceptualizations could be offered to explain why science gets the results it does or why the salmon's tail seems disproportionately narrow, so why do scientists and their followers insist on explaining technological achievements with their particular mythology, and why did the ancient Germanic peoples insist on explaining the morphological traits of fish with theirs? Because, of course, the mythology of science is *sacred* in the modern world, just as the mythology of the heathen Germanic peoples was sacred in their world.

It cannot be emphasized enough that myths are *not*, however, "subjective." We do not arbitrarily choose them. *They* choose *us*, and it is from their having been *disclosed* to us, quite apart from our nitpicking reason, that they derive their sanctity. The whole of our perception points back to them, having proceeded outward from them in the first place.

Many proposed definitions of myth are centrally concerned with a narrative form over a conceptual form, but, as we have seen, this is not what ultimately defines myth. Concepts can be myths just as readily as tales or images can be. Yet there is one decisive way in which conceptual myths differ from those that have the form of stories. Polytheistic myths are located in a vigorous and nuanced engagement with a particular land. Our own lives have the arc of a story, and when we recognize that the trees, the winds, the mountains, the rivers, and the deer who inhabit this same place are characters in these tales, agents in their own right, we begin to perceive the larger, transpersonal stories in which all of us are embedded - the archetypal stories of the land itself. Conceptual language, which has been overwhelmingly favored over the narrative since Socrates, allows for the expression of distance from this awe-ful drama. There is not necessarily any intrinsic property in a conceptual idiom that *creates* such a distance where there was none before, but once such a distance has been established, this more "universal" and impersonal way of speaking can serve as a bulwark to maintain and amplify that distance, to allow monotheists to continue to try to hold themselves aloof from the land.

The irony here is that all myths, even those that seem to build the highest walls to keep the more-than-human world out of our lives, are disclosed to us *by this very world*. They are given to us by the powers who dwell within the land, no matter how much these lands have been shaped by the influence of humankind. For the pre-Christian Germanic peoples, their most common point of origin was in the vast wisdom of Óðinn. One of Óðinn's signature possessions was the enchanted mead Óðrœrir, sips of which he distributed to those humans he deemed worthy of being a true poet or scholar. The names of the god and the mead come from the same word: *óðr* is an Old Norse term that has no equivalent in modern English, but our words "inspiration," "ecstasy," and "fury" all express shades of its meaning. It was the driving force within artistic creativity, mantic trance states, and the frenzy of the battlefield (Old Norse *berserksgangr*, which often involved shifting one's shape into that of a bear or a wolf). *Óðinn* means "Master of *óðr*," and *Óðrœrir* means "Stirrer of *óðr*." Óðinn's gift of his mead, then, was a gift of a corpuscle of his own essence, which intoxicated its recipient with some exceptional insight into the deepest levels of reality and thereby enabled him or her to become a master of the spiritual arts. Thus it should come as no surprise that the two surviving Old Norse poems that have bequeathed to us the richest accounts of indigenous cosmological lore, the *Völuspá* and the *Grímnismál*, are both presented as being orated by a seer or seeress in ecstasy. This sacred, mythical knowledge comes from the gods themselves, and it is not in our everyday, mundane mode of perception that we perceive it the most clearly, but rather in our rarest and most sublime states. It is one of the most dramatic recapitulations of our belonging in this god-haunted world.

Reason

What, then, of reason? Far from being a "check" on myth, reason is as dependent on myth as a newborn is on its mother. It has its place, yes, but its powers are really quite small when pitted against forces as formidable as divine intoxication. The modern cult of reason, which found its most ludicrous expression in the "Temples of Reason" erected throughout France during the French Revolution, is totally unwarranted. All that reason has the capacity to do is deduce new, profane principles from existing myths and suggest ways of acting at the profane levels of life in accordance with existing myths.

Philosophers even have a ready phrase for this "problem:" "infinite regress." Any logical proof must begin with a statement whose validity is assumed *a priori*, for if one were to provide an additional statement to validate the first statement in any given proof, one would then have to validate that statement in turn with another, and that one with another, and so on. Where does this process stop? From an indigenous Germanic perspective, it stops when a myth is reached. This happens effortlessly; there is nothing forced, arbitrary, or "problematic" in it. When Descartes pronounced "I think, therefore I am" to be a self-evident truth that could serve as the initial statement of a proof, he was in effect declaring, "Here is my myth. It has been granted to me by my god, and its impulse is far mightier than my logic. Beyond this point I can question no further." He then proceeded to construct an entire cosmology out of this and other such formative assumptions.

Descartes's rationalism was as "hopelessly" mythical as the worldview of any prehistoric hunter-gatherer. What about the empiricism of Aristotle, Bacon, and their followers? As we have noted, the senses do not sense apart from the intuition, but are informed by it at every turn. Aristotle's attempt to artificially sever the senses from the intuition was, as we have seen, a result of his commitment to the paradoxical myth of the a-mythical profaneness of the world. Myths, after all, reside within the intuition, the *vis phantastica* of the Renaissance philosophers. All of us, including Aristotle, observe the world through the lenses of our myths. Induction still, at bottom, retains some element of myth without which there could be no induction at all, for the visible modality of the world lives on the vivification it receives from its corresponding invisible modality.

Reason's reliance on myth also spoils Aristotle's Law of Noncontradiction - the principle that decrees that the statements "A is B" and "A is not B" cannot both be true. This is a classically monotheistic claim. If there is one god and one standard of truth, and if that standard holds that "A is B" is true, then "A is not B" is naturally condemned to the outer darkness of objective falsehood. But if various gods inspire various myths, "A is B" can be true according to certain myths, and "A is not B" can be true according to others. John Keats called the ability to live in the midst of such competing ideas without attempting to reduce one to another "Negative Capability," and he saw this embrace of volatility as being an indispensable nutrient for creative achievement. After all, are we not immersed in such contradictions every day of our lives? The world provides sustenance and comfort, but it also sickens, wounds, and eventually murders us. Our friends annoy us but remain our friends. Our enemies inspire us but remain our enemies. For a monotheist, this polyvalence is blasphemy, and so the monotheist declares the world a blasphemer and seeks to banish it. For a polytheist, the world is at the height of its singeing, tingling beauty and glory when it is also at the height of its volcanic dynamism. The polytheist *sacralizes* this polyvalence.

Perspectivism

All knowing occurs from a particular position amongst this dynamism, which has tremendous ramifications for what constitutes knowledge and what constitutes delusion. What we see is determined by the vantage point from which we look, and what is true from one position is not true from another - a recognition which Nietzsche called "perspectivism." This should be understood in contrast to relativism, the more or less nihilistic assertion that "anything goes," which is merely the inversion of the Judeo-Christian fetish for absolutes. There is no objective standard of truth to which an idea can be held, but there are countless *perspectival* standards of truth to which an idea can indeed rightly be held. One's perspective on the world is a matter of the position one occupies in the matrix of relationships within which one lives and perceives and thinks. Truth is nestled inside this web of relationships, and as the web changes, so does truth. What is obviously true from one position in the web is just as obviously false from another, and there is nothing awry in this. The world is sufficiently polyvalent to envelop all of these possibilities and more.

The actual is subsumed by the perceptual; in Merleau-Ponty's words, which seem carefully chosen to challenge Descartes, "The certainty of ideas is not the foundation for the certainty of perception but is, rather, based on it. ... In this sense all consciousness is perceptual, even the consciousness of ourselves. ... The perceived thing... exists only insofar as someone can perceive it. I cannot even for an instant imagine an object in itself." To perceive something is to already stand in relation to it, to be a participant in its life and it in one's own, even to have some modicum of agency in shaping its constitution. Truths, like rivers and crickets, are quintessentially worldly things that could not exist as themselves apart from those to whom they stand in relation.

Truths are also inextricable from values. The modern English language contains an implicit recognition of this in the double meaning of the words "right" and "wrong," which can mean, respectively, both "correct" and "good" on the one hand and "incorrect" and "bad" on the other. Thus there should be nothing startling in the realization that the perspectival character of truth extends to aesthetics as well. What qualifies as a fine and invigorating meal from the perspective of a hawk is annihilation from the perspective of the mouse on whom she dines.

Just as the monotheist denies the particularity of truth by insisting on subjecting all perception to an "objective" standard, so he insists on subjecting all aesthetics to a monolithic standard of "good" and "evil." This is what morality is - the monotheist's aesthetics, transposed into a universalist, totalizing idiom. The riotous, astonishing diversity of gods, of truths, of values, is reduced to one god, one truth, and one morality, like a flat plane of pavement where a forest used to flourish.

Nietzsche articulated the esteem for pluralism inherent in polytheism when he said of pre-Christian Europe:

> *One was permitted to behold a plurality of norms; one god was not considered a denial of another god, nor blasphemy against him. It was here that the luxury of individuals was first permitted; it was here that one first honored the rights of individuals. The freedom that one conceded to a god in his relation to other gods - one eventually also granted to oneself in relation to laws, customs, and neighbors. Monotheism on the other hand, this rigid consequence of the doctrine of one human type - the faith in one normal god beside whom there are only pseudo-gods - was perhaps the greatest danger that has yet confronted humanity.*

Examples of this "plurality of norms" among the Germanic divinities are too numerous to count. Where the honor of Þórr and Týr was close to impeccable, Loki and Óðinn had scant regard for such societal conventions and expectations. Loki's mischievous and irreverent playfulness refused to subject itself to such constraints, while Óðinn's quest for personal power and creative agency led him to master feminine forms of magic that brought unspeakable shame and dishonor to most Germanic men who dared to even dabble in them - and yet he was still the chief of the Æsir gods. The Æsir, Vanir, and Jötnar tribes of gods and spirits had highly charged and ambivalent relations with one another that ranged from intermarriage to open war. Where Óðinn was a patron of the socioeconomically, intellectually, and militarily elite, Þórr was a champion of the common people. Even single acts could embody a "plurality of norms," such as when Týr bravely, nobly, and compassionately sacrificed one of his two hands in order to guarantee a false oath that saved the gods from sudden destruction, even though swearing a false oath was commonly viewed as perhaps the most petty and vulgar thing one could do. And so on.

IV.
Destiny

The Turning of Being

Ask veit ek standa,
Heitir Yggdrasils,
Hár baðmr, ausinn
Hvíta auri;
Þaðan koma döggvar,
Þærs í dala falla,
Stendr æ yfir grænn
Urðarbrunni.

Þaðan koma meyjar
Margs vitandi
Þrjár ór þeim sæ,
Er und þolli stendr;
Urð hétu eina,
Aðra Verðandi
- Skáru á skíði, -
Skuld ina þriðju;
Þær lög lögðu,
Þær líf kuru
Alda börnum,
Örlög seggja.

[I know an ash tree standing,
Yggdrasils its name,
Its heights awash
In white hail always;
From there the dewdrops fall

65

That land in deepest vales,
As evergreen it stands
Over Urðr's Well.

From there come maidens
Vastly wise
Three from the lake
That lies beneath the tree;
Urðr one is called,
Verðandi is another,
The third of them is Skuld;
They carve into the wood,
They place what is placed,
They etch the lives
Of every child;
Their laws are first and greatest.]

These verses from the *Völuspá* depict what was perceived to unfold at the very center of the invisible, mythical world of the Germanic tribes. The *axis mundi* around which that world was arranged was called, in Old Norse, *Askr Yggdrasils*, the "Ash Tree of the Steed of the Terrible One" - that is, the shamanic "ladder" that Sleipnir, Óðinn's horse, took to bear his rider between the dwelling-places of the Æsir, Vanir, Jötnar, elves, the dead, and other classes of beings, which were located in the branches and roots of that cosmic tree. (Its more general name seems to have been a lost cognate of Old Saxon *Irminsul* and Old English *Eormensul*, "Mighty

Tree.") Its regal heights were snow-capped, and its lowest roots reached the waters of *Urðarbrunnr*, the "Well of Urðr," which stood at the base of the tree. The denizens of this murky pool were the three *Nornir* ("Cunning Women," "Witches"), Urðr, Verðandi, and Skuld, "vastly wise maidens" who set destiny on its course by carving runes into the trunk of the tree who holds all life in its sprawling arms and legs.

Destiny permeates this image in accordance with the Germanic view of cyclical time. Germanic languages have only two tenses, the past and the present, and express something similar to futurity - which could more accurately be called "necessity," "intention," or "obligation" - through the use of modal verbs in the present tense ("I will go," "it shall be," etc.). Necessity is not a true tense, but is rather an aspect or an outgrowth of the past and present tenses. Urðr's Well, the reservoir of completed actions, corresponds to the past tense, and Askr Yggdrasils, which rises up from the past, corresponds to the present. The sky, toward which the growing tree and the evaporating wellwater are impelled, corresponds to necessity.

The water in the image is constantly in motion. It is taken up by the roots of the tree, nourishing it, sustaining it, and transforming it, and evaporates into the sky. There it freezes, and hail is sprinkled on the tree's branches, while water drips back as dew into the well, sustaining and altering the well in turn. The water cycle is the tangible disclosure of the cycle of time, which originates in the past, feeds the present and the necessary, and then, as the arc of the "future" culminates by falling back to the past, changes the constitution of the past. The new past then proceeds upward into the new present, charged with new obligations.

The three Nornir correspond to these three dimensions of the image. The names "Urðr" and "Verðandi" are both derived from the verb *verða*, "to turn" or "to become," a cognate of the modern German *werden*. "Urðr" comes from a past tense form of the verb, and means "That Which Has Become." "Verðandi" is a present form, and means "That Which is Becoming." Skuld, "Debt," comes from the verb *skulu*, "shall," and can perhaps best be translated as simply "Necessity." *Urðr*, or in Old English *wyrd*, from whence we have the modern English "weird," was often used to denote destiny in its entirety.

These three terrifyingly powerful forces are the authors of the framework of destiny within which all of us whose homelands are found amongst the tree's branches and roots - men, women, gods, mountains, slugs - must, of necessity, live. The range of choices available to us, both in terms of actions and of thoughts, is severely constrained by these three "vastly wise maidens." "Free will" is a laughable idea in the face of their preeminence. But neither are our possibilities wholly determined, as in Aristotle's linear, mechanistic cause and effect, or its modern recapitulation in the insistence that the motivations of nonhuman life are purely instinctual. Destiny flows through us on its way into the present and back to the past, and we have the ability to harness and direct it along the way, like a bird riding the wind. We do not, however, get to choose which way the wind blows.

Our selfhood is our place in the flows and cycles of destiny. Just as many ecologists (who, like Darwin, are sometimes a refreshing counterweight to the dominant mythology of science) describe all life as being interconnected by a web, so destiny was often imagined as a web in the heathen Germanic religion, as in the *Darraðarljóð*, for example. Being, like knowledge, is inherently relational. We are ourselves and not anything else because we exist in relation to others in the past and the present, from our most distant ancestors to the most recent of acquaintances, in specific ways. Somewhat paradoxically, our particularity is a matter of our *bonds*, in both senses of the word - our relationships and our constraints or obligations. Based on a fundamentally identical intuition, Heidegger preferred to speak of a "being-in-the-world" (German *in-der-Welt-sein*) rather than simply a "being." Merleau-Ponty went further and described perception as an "intertwining" between perceiver and perceived wherein both have agency in shaping the other. The rabbit knows that her selfhood is edible because she is perceived as prey by the mountain lion; the lion, meanwhile, is reminded of his status as a predator when, even when he is satiated and exhausted, he sees the rabbits hiding or fleeing from him. Both have acquired their ontological condition by this perceptual engagement and its definitive role in matters of life and death.

Destiny works to fulfill the archetypal myths of the land, the Eternal Circle of birth, life, death, and rebirth. Our lives have meaning and purpose by virtue of their being swept up in this greater rhythm. It should go without saying that this is not, fundamentally, a purpose we choose, nor is it a purpose that will somehow ensure that "everything will work out in the end" for our benefit. Our particularity as destined beings-in-the-world also bears little resemblance to the precious chimera of "individuality," and we possess nothing as aloof and invulnerable as a "soul." We are weather patterns, flitting in and out of existence as blithely and with as little consequence as a cloud. But can we not help but marvel, at least every now and then, at the scandalous beauty of existence, what Robinson Jeffers called the "transhuman magnificence" of the world? To feel the ecstasy of manifesting some crumb of this grandeur, of propelling the world's tireless creation and re-creation *of itself*, which has no beginning and no end?

The Eternal Circle

What are these archetypal myths at destiny's heart? They are the tales that comprise the great mythological cycle of the Germanic tribes and their correspondences in the storied worldviews of many of the world's other polytheistic peoples, past and present. They narrate the first emergence of the cosmos, its flourishing and climax, and its dissolution back into primal chaos, out of which the cosmos inexorably crawls once again.

The cycle began, as we have noted, with the perfect stillness and emptiness of Ginnungagap. On either side of Ymir's abyss lay the last refuges of elemental ice and fire, the only remaining ruins of the cosmos. The rime and flames expanded until they met, hissing and sputtering, within the void. Like a seed that had been biding its time beneath the frost, Búri ("Father"), the progenitor of the Æsir, came out from the warming ice. Ymir and Búri were both hermaphrodites, and gave birth to their sons and daughters in solitude. Búri sired Borr ("Son"), and Ymir Bölþorn ("Baleful Thorn"), who in turn fathered Bestla ("Wife"). Borr and Bestla mated and gave birth to Óðinn, Vili, and Vé. Through their birth, the forces of life and the forces of death became intertwined, and the eventual succumbing of the former to the latter was intimated, even this early in the drama.

But by this point the new cosmos was still mostly innocent, and had just begun to take shape. Óðinn and his brothers furthered this process by slaying Ymir and forming the visible world from his corpse, as we have seen. The Æsir established their stronghold, Ásgarðr, in the upper branches of Askr Yggdrasils. Constant incursions by the Jötnar were a fact of life, but their fortress and their well-being were more than amply protected by the strength and temper of Þórr and the vigilance of their watchman Heimdallr.

One from their ranks, Loki, mated with the jötunn Angrboða ("She Who Bodes Anguish"), and from their union came three of the most dreadful monstrosities in the world: Hel ("Grave"), the death goddess; Jörmungandr ("Great Beast of Sorcery"), the sea serpent who encircles the land; and Fenrir ("He Who Lives in the Fens"), a wolf stronger than any of the gods. Hel was tossed into the soil, and Jörmungandr into the ocean. But Fenrir filled the gods with such foreboding that they reared him within Ásgarðr so that they could watch and control him. He grew at an astonishing and terrifying speed, however, and soon the gods decided that the only prudent course of action was to bind him and leave him in some desolate, solitary place where he could bring no harm to anyone. The gods fashioned chain after chain, each one more tenacious than the one before, and they convinced the wolf to allow them to place the fetters around him under the pretext of proving his might. Fenrir snapped free of each in turn. At last the dwarves forged a magical chain from the footfalls of a cat, the spittle of a bird, and the roots of a mountain. Although it was the sturdiest manacle in the cosmos, it was slight and even silky in appearance, which made Loki's son suspicious. He refused to be bound with it unless one of the gods would place his or her hand in his mouth as a pledge of good faith. Only Týr was brave and loyal enough to fulfill this request, and when the wolf was unable to escape, he duly tore Týr's hand from its wrist. Týr's hand was not all that he sacrificed, however; according to ancient northern European tradition, this blemish would have rendered him unfit to rule alongside Óðinn, not to mention the dishonor of oath-breaking. The bound Fenrir was cast into a bog, far enough from Ásgarðr that the gods would not be troubled by the echoes of his incessant, enraged howling, and a sword was placed in his mouth to pacify his jaws. His drool became a foamy river, whose name, Ván ("Expectation"), hinted that destiny had more in store for the wolf.

Around this time, Baldr ("Bold") reached the height of his powers. His fame as a warrior, charm, and bright face made him the most beloved of all of Óðinn's many sons. When he began to be troubled by dreams portending his death, his mother, Frigg, went to every living thing and secured oaths from them to let no harm come to her son. Baldr had been in an long-standing and unresolved feud with Höðr ("Warrior") over the goddess Nanna (perhaps "Daring"), whose hand in marriage was yearned for by both. One day, when the Æsir were amusing themselves by throwing whatever they could find at Baldr and watching it bounce off his uninjured body, Loki, guileful trickster that he was, sensed an opportunity for mischief. He approached Frigg in disguise and asked her whether *everything* had sworn the oath she had requested, or if anything had been omitted. Frigg casually replied that only the mistletoe had failed to swear the oath, but she was unconcerned by this due to the mistletoe's being such a small and harmless thing. Loki flew to the mistletoe and carved a spear out of it, which he handed to Höðr, informing him that this was the only weapon in the world that could dispatch his enemy, but that if he were to use it, Nanna would assuredly be his.

Höðr approached the ring of revelers and hurled the spear at the shining god, who, to the shock and horror of all who were present, fell down dead on the spot. After the gods came to their senses, they drove away Höðr and Loki, and sent one of Baldr's brothers, Hermóðr ("War-passion") to Hel to see if there was any possibility of the retrieval of their fallen companion. After Sleipnir bore him down the trunk of Askr Yggdrasils and to the dark, earthen home of Hel, Hermóðr pleaded with the stone-faced goddess for the release of his brother, telling her of the anguish of all the living over the absence of the bright god. At last Hel consented to this much: that if every living being would weep for him, she would allow him to return to Ásgarðr. Hermóðr brought this desperate news to Frigg, who went about as she had done before, this time winning tears from all life - all, that is, except for one jötunn, Þökk ("Thanks"), who was surely none other than Loki in another one of his disguises. And so Baldr remained in Hel's cold clutches.

Loki had fled with a livid Þórr in close pursuit. He managed to elude the thunder god long enough to hide in a river in the form of a salmon, but he was ultimately captured and taken to a cave. The gods brought his two sons to the cave, transformed one of them into a wolf, and had him murder his brother right there before Loki's eyes. With the entrails of his dead son, the gods bound Loki to a boulder and placed a venomous snake above his head to drip poison onto his face. His wife, Sigyn ("Victory-friend"), was as faithful as Loki was devious, and enabled him to escape some portion of the gods' punishment by sitting at his side with a bowl to catch the poison as it fell. When the bowl would fill, however, she would have to leave the cave to empty it, and the drops that reached Loki's face caused the god to writhe so violently that they created earthquakes.

But as the wheel of destiny turned, Loki and Fenrir broke free of their chains. A winter as long and ploddingly harsh as any three that had come before ensorcelled the world. The great tree trembled and groaned. Ragnarök (the "Doom of the Gods," also occasionally spelled *Ragnarökkr*, "Twilight of the Gods") had begun.

From his post above the gates of Ásgarðr, Heimdallr spied Naglfar ("Death-ship"), the warship of the jötnar, heading swiftly for the gods' castle with none other than Loki at the helm. The gods fought as bravely and nobly as any human heroes whose songs have ever been sung, but they were no match for their own destiny. Þórr fell to Jörmungandr, Óðinn and Týr to

Fenrir, and Freyr to Surtr ("Black"), whose fiery sword swept across the earth, leaving nothing but charcoal and ash in its wake. Fenrir ran across the earth with his lower jaw on the ground and his upper jaw in the heavens, devouring everything in his path - even swallowing the sun, the moon, and the stars. The last light the world ever saw was Surtr's fire. The black land sank back into the sea, whose waves closed over it and fell silent, and Ginnungagap prevailed once more.

But, in time, fire and ice found each other again, and even Baldr returned to gladden the buzzing forests and meadows.

This tale is the story of stories, the foundational myth from which all of life acquires its shape, its trajectory, and its meaning. The "Twilight of the Gods" is manifested in every twilight, every autumn, every waning moon, every collapse of a civilization, every death, every wildfire, every mass extinction. Baldr reaches the height of his powers in every noon, summer, full moon, peak of a civilization, prime of life, and "climax community." The story repeats itself at all scales and throughout all time; all of life is a revelation of some sliver of this divine, demonic mystery that lies at its heart. Everything that belongs to what we call "history," this profane particularity of events and of beings that seems to follow a linear path when considered in isolation from the loam from which it grows, will crumble into nothingness. Even memory can only last so long. We in our superfluous historicity do not recur eternally. But the gods, the archetypal beings of whom we embody some small and incomplete part, and the cycle of *their* lives, *are* truly eternal, brimming with infinite significance, and worthy of nothing but unconditional - if sometimes necessarily painful and strained - affirmation: *amor fati*, the love of destiny. We do not have to search for meaning in life; just being alive is meaning enough in and of itself.

Glossary of Old Norse Words

Æsir: One of the two main tribes of deities, the other one being the Vanir.

Angrboða: A female jötunn, with whom Loki sired Fenrir, Hel, and Jörmungandr.

Ásgarðr: Usually Anglicized "Asgard." It is the stronghold of the Æsir gods and goddesses, located in the upper branches of Askr Yggdrasils.

Askr Yggdrasils: The central pillar of the cosmos; the world-tree that grows out of Urðarbrunnr. All living beings dwell in its branches and roots. Its name is often given as "Yggdrasil" or "Yggdrasill," but *Askr Yggdrasils* is its full and more proper name.

Baldr: The most widely beloved of all of the Æsir gods, a son of Óðinn and Frigg. He was killed by Höðr and Loki and forced to remain in Hel until Ragnarök. He was probably thought of as being the animating spirit of life at the peak of its strength and beauty. There are two full accounts of his death: that of Snorri Sturluson and that of Saxo Grammaticus. For Snorri, Baldr is an innocent sufferer, whereas for Saxo he is a fierce warrior fighting with Höðr over their love of the goddess Nanna, which seems truer to the warlike character of the Germanic peoples and their gods. I have included elements from both versions in my own retelling.

berserksgangr: "Going berserk," being overcome with óðr and raging, nigh-invincible, through battle. *Berserk* means "bear-shirt," and is almost certainly a reference to shapeshifting into a bear, a common occurrence amongst those possessed by óðr in the sagas.

Bestla: A female jötunn, the daughter of Bölþorn, and the mother of Óðinn, Vili, and Vé.

Bölþorn: A jötunn, probably the son of Ymir, and the father of Bestla.

Borr: An Æsir god, the son of Búri and the father of Óðinn, Vili, and Vé.

Búri: The father of Borr and the progenitor of the Æsir.

Darraðarljóð: A poem contained within *Njal's Saga*. On the eve of the Battle of Clontarf, the Norns (who are glossed as valkyries) are spied weaving the destiny of the battle and all who will partake in it. They use intestines for the thread, severed heads for the weights, and swords and arrows for beaters.

Fenrir: The wolf son of Loki and Angrboða who powerfully assists the destruction of the world during Ragnarök, killing both Óðinn and Týr along the way.

Freyr: "Lord," one of the foremost of the Vanir deities, who falls to Surtr during Ragnarök.

Frigg: An Æsir goddess, the wife of Óðinn, and the loving and devoted mother of Baldr.

Ginnungagap: The primordial abyss that was all that existed prior to the emergence of the cosmos.

Grímnismál: One of the central poems contained in the medieval collection called the "Poetic Edda."

Hermóðr: An Æsir god and son of Óðinn who rode down to Hel to attempt to retrieve Baldr after that god's death.

Höðr: A god who slew Baldr as part of a feud over the love of the goddess Nanna (according to Saxo, whose version differs from the more commonly repeated account by Snorri).

Jörmungandr: Often Anglicized as "Jormungand." He is the sea serpent who encircles the land on earth and slays

Þórr during Ragnarök. Loki and Angrboða are his parents.

Jötnar: A tribe of spirits who are often spuriously called "giants" in books on Norse mythology. The word *Jötnar* translates to "Devourers," and they are seldom, if ever, portrayed as being especially large in size (not in any reliable primary sources, at least). Their distinguishing feature is their being forces of chaos, night, winter, cold, and death, and also of the wilderness and primal wisdom. Their relationship with the two tribes of gods, the Æsir and the Vanir, is highly ambiguous. The "Devourers" and the gods are often enemies, yet they often intermarry and have other sorts of friendly relations. During Ragnarök, however, the Æsir defend the cosmos, while the Jötnar destroy it. While they are not usually considered gods *per se*, they were every bit as powerful as the gods, and received worship during the Viking Age and probably much farther back as well.

jötunn: One of the Jötnar.

Loki: The wily trickster of the Æsir, whose mischief brings more harm than good. He is the father of Fenrir, Jörmungandr, and Hel, and aids the Jötnar during Ragnarök.

Naglfar: "Ship of the Dead," the ship by which the Jötnar reach Ásgarðr during Ragnarök.

Nanna: The wife of Baldr, also loved covetously by Höðr.

Nornir: The three animating spirits of destiny.

Óðinn: Usually Anglicized as "Odin." He is the chief of the Æsir, the husband of Frigg, and the animating spirit of óðr.

óðr: A word with no direct English equivalent, which has been variously translated as "inspiration," "ecstasy," and "furor." It is a mystical power granted by Óðinn that imparts great creative agency in artistic, spiritual, and military pursuits.

Óðrœrir: The mead of óðr.

Ragnarök: The downfall of the cosmos and its sinking back into the formless chaos of Ginnungagap.

Sigyn: Loki's wife, who stays by his side and aids him during his imprisonment in the cave after the death of Baldr.

Skuld: One of the three Nornir, whose name means "Necessity."

Sleipnir: Óðinn's eight-legged shamanic steed, who bears him and other gods from Ásgarðr to the underworld and various other places within the branches and roots of Askr Yggdrasils.

Surtr: A jötunn with a flaming sword who burns the world during Ragnarök.

Þjazi: A jötunn who, in a tale not recounted in this work, kidnaps a goddess.

Þökk: A jötunn, surely Loki in disguise, who refuses to weep for Baldr, thus ensuring that he will remain in the underworld until the cosmos is reborn after Ragnarök.

Þórr: "Thunder," usually Anglicized as Thor. He is one of the foremost of the Æsir gods, a son of Óðinn, and a stalwart defender of the cosmos against the Jötnar.

Týr: "God," one of the rulers of the Æsir gods and especially associated with law and justice. His hand is bitten off by Fenrir after it was placed in the wolf's mouth to secure a false oath. In Ragnarök, Fenrir finishes him off.

Urðarbrunnr: The "Well of Urðr" or "Well of Destiny" beneath the roots of Askr Yggdrasils.

Urðr: One of the three Nornir, whose name means "That Which Has Become." *Urðr* is also often used to refer to destiny as a whole.

Ván: The foamy river that flows from the mouth of the bound Fenrir.

Vanir: One of the two main tribes of deities, the other being the Æsir. The Vanir were especially associated with the fertility of humans and the more-than-human world, and were known for their debauchery and hedonism as well as their power, beauty, and innocence.

Vé: One of Óðinn's brothers who aids in the creation of the visible world from Ymir's corpse. He is almost certainly a hypostasis of Óðinn.

Verðandi: One of the three Nornir, "That Which is Becoming."

Vili: One of Óðinn's brothers who aids in the creation of the visible world from Ymir's corpse. He is almost certainly a hypostasis of Óðinn.

Völuspá: One of the central poems in the medieval collection known as the "Poetic Edda." It may be the single most important and comprehensive source for our current knowledge of Norse mythology relative to its reliability.

Ymir: The first living being and the progenitor of the Jötnar. He was slain by Óðinn, Vili, and Vé, who crafted the visible world from his corpse.

Selected Bibliography

Abram, David. 1991. "The Mechanical and the Organic: On the Impact of Metaphor in Science." In *Scientists on Gaia*, edited by Stephen Schneider and Penelope Boston. M.I.T. Press: Cambridge, MA.

Abram, David. 1996. *The Spell of the Sensuous: Perception and Language in a More-than-human World.* Random House, Inc.: New York, NY.

Abram, David. 2004. *Reciprocity.* In *Rethinking Nature: Essays in Environmental Philosophy.* Edited by Bruce V. Foltz and Robert Frodeman. Indiana University Press: Bloomington, IN.

Abram, David. 2010. *Becoming Animal: An Earthly Cosmology.* Pantheon Books: New York, NY.

Adam of Bremen. 2002. *The History of the Archbishops of Hamburg-Bremen.* Translated by Francis Joseph Tschan. Columbia University Press: New York, NY.

Anonymous. *The Poetic Edda.* In original Old Norse at http://www.heimskringla.no/wiki/eddukvæði.

Anonymous. 2000. *Beowulf.* Translated by Seamus Heaney. W.W. Norton & Company: New York, NY.

Bates, Brian. 2005. *The Way of Wyrd*. Hay House: Carlsbad, CA.

Bauschatz, Paul C. 1978. *The Germanic Ritual Feast*. In *The Nordic Languages and Modern Linguistics 3*. Edited by John Weinstock. University of Texas Press: Austin, TX.

Bauschatz, Paul C. 1982. *The Well and the Tree: World and Time in Early Germanic Culture*. University of Massachusetts Press: Amherst, MA.

Bird-David, Nurit. 1999. *"Animism" Revisited: Personhood, Environment, and Relational Epistemology*. In *Current Anthropology* 40.

Blake, William. 1988. *The Complete Poetry and Prose of William Blake*. Edited by David V. Erdman. Random House: New York, NY.

Branston, Brian. 1957. *The Lost Gods of England*. Thames and Hudson: London, UK.

Bruno, Giordano. 1998. *On Bonding in a General Sense*. In *Cause, Principle, and Unity: and Essays on Magic*. Edited and translated by Richard J. Blackwell. Cambridge University Press: Cambridge, UK.

Byock, Jesse L. (trans.). 2000. *The Saga of the Volsungs*. Penguin Books: New York, NY.

Chadwick, H.M. 1899. *The Cult of Othin*. C.J. Clay and Sons: London, UK.

Couliano, Ioan P. 1987. *Eros and Magic in the Renaissance*. University of Chicago Press: Chicago, IL.

Dawkins, Richard. 2004. *A Devil's Chaplain: Reflections on Hope, Lies, Science, and Love*. Mariner Books: New York, NY.

De Benoist, Alain. 2004. *On Being a Pagan*. Edited by Greg Johnson. Translated by Jon Graham. Ultra: Atlanta, GA.

Deloria, Vine. 1992. *God is Red: a Native View of Religion*. Fulcrum: Golden, CO.

Deloria, Vine. 1995. *Red Earth, White Lies: Native Americans and the Myth of Scientific Fact*. Scribner: New York, NY.

Deloria, Vine. 2006. *The World We Used to Live In: Remembering the Powers of the Medicine Men*. Fulcrum: Golden, CO.

Deloria, Vine. 2008. *Interview*. In *How Shall I Live My Life?: On Liberating the Earth from Civilization*. Edited by Derrick Jensen. PM Press: Oakland, CA.

Descartes, René. 1997. *Key Philosophical Writings*. Translated by Elizabeth S. Haldane and G.R.T. Ross. Edited by Enrique Chávez Arizo. Wordsworth Editions Limited: Ware, UK.

DuBois, Thomas. 1999. *Nordic Religions in the Viking Age*. University of Pennsylvania Press: Philadelphia, PA.

Dumézil, Georges. 1973. *Gods of the Ancient Northmen.* University of California Press: Los Angeles, CA.

Dumézil, Georges. 1988. *Mitra-Varuna: an Essay on Two Indo-European Representations of Sovereignty.* Zone Books: New York, NY.

Easla, Brian. 1980. *Witch-Hunting, Magic, and the New Philosophy: and Introduction to Debates of the Scientific Revolution, 1450-1750.* The Harvester Press Limited: Brighton, UK.

Eliade, Mircea. 1951. *Shamanism: Archaic Techniques of Ecstasy.* Trans. Willard Trask. Princeton University Press: Princeton, NJ.

Eliade, Mircea. 1957. *The Sacred and the Profane: the Nature of Religion.* Trans. Willard Trask. Harcourt: Orlando, FL.

Eliade, Mircea. 1959. *Cosmos and History: the Myth of the Eternal Return.* Harper & Row: New York, NY.

Ellis-Davidson, H.R. 1964. *Gods and Myths of Northern Europe.* Penguin Books: New York, NY.

Ellis-Davidson, H.R. 1967. *Pagan Scandinavia.* F.A. Praeger: New York, NY.

Ellis-Davidson, H.R. 1968. *The Road to Hel: a Study of the Conception of the Dead in Old Norse Literature.* Greenwood: Abingdon, UK.

Ellis-Davidson, H.R. 1988. *Myths and Symbols in Pagan Europe: Early Scandinavian and Celtic Religions.* Syracuse University Press: Syracuse, NY.

Ellis-Davidson, H.R. 1993. *The Lost Beliefs of Northern Europe.* Routledge: New York, NY.

Enright, Michael J. 1995. *Lady with a Mead Cup: Ritual Prophecy and Lordship in the European Warband from La Tène to the Viking Age.* Four Courts Press: Dublin, Ireland.

Flowers, Stephen E. 1986. *Runes and Magic: Magical Formulaic Elements in the Older Runic Tradition.* University of Texas Press: Austin, TX.

Graves, Robert. 1948. *The White Goddess: A Historical Grammar of Poetic Myth.* Farrar, Straus and Giroux: New York, NY.

Greer, John Michael. 2005. *A World Full of Gods: an Inquiry into Polytheism.* ADF Publishing: Tucson, AZ.

Gundarsson, Kveldulf. 2007. *Elves, Wights, and Trolls.* iUniverse: Lincoln, NE.

Hallowell, A. Irving. 1960. *Ojibwe Ontology, Behavior, and World View.* In *Culture in History: Essays in Honor of Paul Radin.* Edited by Stanley Diamond. Columbia University Press: New York, NY.

Harvey, Graham. 2005. *Animism: Respecting the Living World.* Columbia University Press: New York, NY.

Hatab, Lawrence J. 1990. *Myth and Philosophy: a Contest of Truths.* Open Court: La Salle, Illinois.

Heidegger, Martin. 1962. *Being and Time.* Trans. John Macquarrie and Edward Robinson. Harper & Row: New York, NY.

Heidegger, Martin. 1971. *Poetry, Language, Thought.* Ed. and trans. Albert Hofstadter. Harper & Row: New York, NY.

Howell, Signe. 1996. *Nature in Culture or Culture in Nature?: Chewong Ideas of 'Humans' and Other Species.* In *Nature and Society: Anthropological Perspectives,* edited by Philippe Descola and Gísli Pálsson. Routledge: London, UK.

Jeffers, Robinson. 1927. *The Selected Poetry of Robinson Jeffers.* Random House, Inc.: New York, NY.

Jensen, Derrick. 2000. *A Language Older than Words.* Chelsea Green: White River Junction, VT.

Jensen, Derrick. 2011. *Dreams.* Seven Stories: New York, NY.

Keats, John. 2002. *Selected Letters.* Edited by Robert Gittings. Oxford University Press: Oxford, UK.

Kershaw, Kris. 2000. *The One-Eyed God: Odin and the (Indo-)Germanic Männerbünde.* Institute for the Study of Man: Washington, DC.

Kure, Henning. 2003. *In the Beginning was the Scream: Conceptual Thought in the Old Norse Myth of Creation.* In *Scandinavia and Christian Europe in the Middle Ages: Papers of the 12th International Saga Conference.* Edited by Rudolf Simek and Judith Meuer. p. 311-319.

Kure, Henning. 2006. *Hanging on the World Tree: Man and Cosmos in Old Norse Mythic Poetry.* In *Old Norse Religion in Long-Term Perspectives: Origins, Changes, and Interactions.* Edited by Anders Andrén, Kristina Jennbert, and Catharina Raudvere. Nordic Academic Press: Lund, Sweden.

Lindow, John. 2001. *Norse Mythology: A Guide to the Gods, Heroes, Rituals, and Beliefs.* Oxford University Press: New York, NY.

Lorde, Audre. 1978. *Poetry is Not a Luxury.* In *Power, Oppression, and the Politics of Culture: a Lesbian/Feminist Perspective.* Out and Out Press: New York, NY.

Maritain, Jacques. 1944. *The Dream of Descartes.* F. Hubner & Co., Inc.: New York, NY.

Merleau-Ponty, Maurice. 1962. *The Phenomenology of Perception.* Trans. Colin Smith. Routledge: New York, NY.

Merleau-Ponty, Maurice. 1964. *The Primacy of Perception: and Other Essays on Phenomenological Psychology, the Philosophy of Art, History, and Politics.* Ed. James M. Edie. Northwestern University Press: Evanston, IL.

Merleau-Ponty, Maurice. 1968. *The Visible and the Invisible.* Ed. John Wild, trans. Alphonso Lingis. Northwestern University Press: Evanston, IL.

Narby, Jeremy. 2005. *Intelligence in Nature: an Inquiry into Knowledge.* Penguin: New York, NY.

Nelson, Richard K. 1983. *Make Prayers to the Raven: a Koyukon View of the Northern Forest.* University of Chicago Press: Chicago, IL.

Nietzsche, Friedrich. 1954. *On Truth and Lie in an Extra-moral Sense.* In *The Portable Nietzsche*, ed. and trans. Walter Kaufmann. The Viking Press: New York, NY.

Nietzsche, Friedrich. 1954. *The Antichrist.* In *The Portable Nietzsche*, ed. and trans. Walter Kaufmann. The Viking Press: New York, NY.

Nietzsche, Friedrich. 1954. *Thus Spoke Zarathustra: a Book for All and None.* In *The Portable Nietzsche*, ed. and trans. Walter Kaufmann. The Viking Press: New York, NY.

Nietzsche, Friedrich. 1954. *Twilight of the Idols, or, How to Philosophize with a Hammer.* In *The Portable Nietzsche*, ed. and trans. Walter Kaufmann. Viking Penguin Inc.: New York, NY.

Nietzsche, Friedrich. 1967. *Beyond Good and Evil: Prelude to a Philosophy of the Future.* In *The Basic*

Writings of Nietzsche, ed. and trans. Walter Kaufmann. Modern Library: New York, NY.

Nietzsche, Friedrich. 1967. *The Birth of Tragedy out of the Spirit of Music*. In *Basic Writings of Nietzsche*, ed. and trans. Walter Kaufmann. Modern Library: New York, NY.

Nietzsche, Friedrich. 1968. *The Will to Power*. Ed. Walter Kaufmann, trans. Walter Kaufmann & R.J. Hollingdale. Random House: New York, NY.

Nietzsche, Friedrich. 1974. *The Gay Science*. Ed. and trans. Walter Kaufmann. Random House: New York, NY.

Olson, Charles. 1950. *Selected Writings*. Ed. Robert Creeley. New Directions: New York, NY.

Price, Neil S. 2002. *The Viking Way: Religion and War in Late Iron Age Scandinavia*. The Department of Archaeology and Ancient History: Uppsala, Sweden.

Raudvere, Catharina. 2002. Trolldómr *in Early Medieval Scandinavia*. In *Witchcraft and Magic in Europe, Vol. 3: The Middle Ages*. Ed. Bengt Ankarloo and Stuart Clark. University of Pennsylvania Press: Philadelphia, PA.

Roszak, Theodore. 1986. *The Cult of Information: the Folklore of Computers and the True Art of Thinking*. Pantheon Books: New York, NY.

Saxo Grammaticus. 2008. *The History of the Danes, Books I-IX*. Ed. H.R. Ellis-Davidson, trans. Peter Fisher. D.S. Brewer: Rochester, NY.

Simek, Rudolf. 1993. *Dictionary of Northern Mythology*. Trans. Angela Hall. D.S. Brewer: Cambridge, UK.

Snorri Sturluson. 1991. *Heimskringla: eða Sögur Noregs Konunga*. In original Old Norse at: http://www.heimskringla.no/wiki/Heimskringla

Snorri Sturluson. 2005. *The Prose Edda*. In original Old Norse   at: http://www.heimskringla.no/wiki/Edda_Snorra_Sturlus onar

Steinsland, Gro. 1987. *Giants as Recipients of Cult in the Viking Age?* In *Words and Objects: Towards a Dialogue between Archaeology and History of Religion*. Edited by Gro Steinsland. p. 212-222.

Tacitus, Cornelius. 1948. *The Agricola and the Germania*. Trans. Harold Mattingly. Penguin Books: New York, NY.

Turville-Petre, Edward Oswald Gabriel. 1964. *Myth and Religion of the North: the Religion of Ancient Scandinavia*. Holt, Rinehart, and Winston: New York, NY.

Viveiros de Castro, Eduardo. 1998. *Cosmological Deixis and Amerindian Perspectivism*. In *The Journal of the Royal Anthropological Institute: Vol. 4, No. 3.*

Viveiros de Castro, Eduardo. 2012. *Cosmological Perspectivism in Amazonia and Elsewhere.* Masterclass Series 1. HAU Network of Ethnographic Theory: Manchester, UK.

White, Lynn, Jr. 1967. *The Historical Roots of Our Ecological Crisis.* In *Science: Vol. 155, No. 3767.*

Wilby, Emma. 2005. *Cunning Folk and Familiar Spirits: Shamanistic Visionary Traditions in Early Modern British Witchcraft and Magic.* Sussex Academic Press: Portland, OR.

Willerslev, Rane. 2007. *Soul Hunters: Hunting, Animism, and Personhood among the Siberian Yukaghirs.* University of California Press: Berkeley and Los Angeles, CA.